POWER

by Paul Anderson

Power By Paul
by Paul Anderson

For Worldwide Distribution
Printed in the U.S.A.

ISBN 0-9772573-3-9

Paul Anderson Youth Home, Inc.
P.O. Box 525 • Vidalia, Georgia 30475

TABLE OF CONTENTS

NOTICE

Please read before starting to consult this course. First, a few "Whys" as to the layout and confirmation of these instructions.

It is bound by this method so it can be opened on a table or bench in the particular section that you are studying and consequently will not have pressure on the pages to fold over to other sections. There is room on each page so that you may make notes or use them for charts. The double spacing is for the same purpose.

Note: Photos and manuscript come from archival materials originally created by the late Paul Anderson in 1974.

INTRODUCTION

In my advertisement for this strength course I used the phrase *"Father of Modern Power Lifting"* as I was discussing my qualifications for such a course. Let me qualify my presumptuousness in using such a description by saying that I do believe that I can rightfully claim such a title because of my knowledge and experience in power lifting.

To give a little background concerning my experience in power lifting, and also to reflect the attitudes of others toward my using the power lifts to strengthen my body, let's go back to my first experience in lifting. As has been stated in my previous courses and articles, I started lifting weights in college to be a better football player, and not with ambition to claim international fame as a strong man. These first efforts were so successful that going into lifting was almost a natural course of events. Also printed before is the fact that the first lift I tried was a deep knee bend. The bench press and the dead lift were the next movements I took up.

When my efforts in lifting first came to the attention of the "experts" of the day, many of them made a real plea for me to stop the useless power movements and concentrate only on doing the three Olympic lifts. Their idea was that I had enough natural strength already, and to build strength for the overhead lifts one should do nothing but these overhead movements. This would not only continue my strength growth, they told me, but would give me form in the Olympic movements.

Being somewhat opinionated, I rejected their free advice and even though I had ambition to prevail in the three Olympic lifts, I felt that the best way to be good at winning international contests was to be strong, and the way to be strong was to do the power lifts that would strengthen the larger muscle groups of the body.

The first time I had an opportunity to go overseas as a representative of my country was in 1955. On this international debut as a heavyweight weightlifter, I had the opportunity to visit many countries and see training methods of those who then prevailed as lifting powers and some who had dominated the sport in the past. Our first stop was in the Soviet Union where there was no sparing of expense when it came to providing training facilities for their lifters and all other athletes. The first training we did was in one of the clubs in Moscow, and there we entered a room with platform after platform where the lifters did their training. All that was in sight was nicely chromed Olympic sets on each platform and an accompanying box holding the magnesium carbonate "chalk" to put on the hands to secure the grip on the barbell. My first reaction was to ask where the rest of the training facilities were, but I soon found that this was it. All the Russian lifters did was to work on the three Olympic lifts, and did nothing else.

Having the desire to get in a couple of good training sessions before my first competition there, I asked the Soviet lifting coaches if it would be possible for me to take some of their weights and set them up in some special positions for different types of training. Being gracious hosts, they allowed me to do this, and were actually very cooperative by helping in any way that they could toward my efforts.

I was real fortunate to spot a piece of equipment that was a great start for rigging up a squat rack and a rack for doing bench presses. This was some type of chinning bar and apparatus to do other such light acrobatics on. I had it moved into position and by doing some taping and adjusting, built a squat rack and bench press station. The Russians were amazed at this procedure on my part, and one time even gathered around in friendly protest as I loaded one of their barbells to 700 pounds for deep knee bends. They felt that the bar could possibly break and result in injuries.

From Russia we went on to the Middle East, and were especially interested in not only our competition against the Egyptian team, but to work out in their facilities there. The story was just about the same as it had been in Moscow. There were no squat racks, and I had some of my teammates assist me in raising a heavy weight to my shoulders to perform deep knee bends there, which resulted in putting a bend in one of their valued Olympic barbells. Their lack of squatting facilities seemed quite strange to me, since some of the earlier squat style Olympic lifters were Egyptians.

Two months later when we gathered in Munich, Germany for the world championships, I noticed a real change in the Russian team's attitude toward training. They had their lifters doing deep knee bends and bench presses and not only high pulls with the barbells as I had done in Moscow, but also stiff-legged dead lifts that I had performed there to keep my lower back in good condition and gain strength. Through the years I have tried to promote power lifting as an enhancement for other sports abilities and the record is quite clear concerning my efforts to convince our athletic coaches to allow their teams to do the deep knee bends for their athletes' speed and agility. There has been much opposition in this field, but we have prevailed in most cases.

Not meaning to sound egotistical, these are some of the reasons that I feel I have been successful in introducing power lifting to the modern-day athlete, and also why I think that I am qualified to write this course.

I hope some of the things you are going to read will be unique and new to you. I am sure they will not all be just that, for some of them are things that I have introduced before in publications, and some that I have passed along to other individuals who have themselves written articles and books on power lifting and lifting for the athlete.

As I always try to emphasize in every instruction that I give, we get out of our movements and exercises just about what we put in. That is, if we approach our exercise routine in a real sincere way, we are going to reach our potentials in just the same way that we trained.

I am including a chapter here that I hope will continue to be of benefit to those interested in lifting. It is a chapter on nutrition, taken from an original course I wrote called "Secrets Of My Strength."

I make a most sincere request before you start a training program from this course. READ ALL OF THE COURSE FIRST.

Chapter 1

NUTRITION

As stated in the introduction, most of the history and ideas in this chapter are taken from "Secrets Of My Strength." I don't have a great deal to add to it, since it was originally complete. I have continued to experiment with high protein foods through the years, and developed several new varieties that I used along with others that are documented here. I have received some fine results from various protein foods mixed with citrus acid and other ingredients, which seem to work quite well.

Chapter 2
DIETS

I began this book on physical power with diets, because this is the first thing that played an active role in my quest for health and physical achievement. When I left the hospital at the age of five and one-half, my doctors instructed my parents concerning my diet. This was a very rigid schedule on which I was to convalesce. Since the disease that put me under the doctors' care had to do with a kidney ailment, this diet was quite strict and minus a great deal of protein. Because my disease had been almost unto death – and I firmly believe only prayers saved my life – my parents were very zealous to see that I followed the doctors' instructions.

Weeks and even months went by without any real improvements in my weakened condition. Fruit juices, starches, and other foods greatly lacking in high quality proteins, although they have a place in our diet, were just not getting the job done. My muscles, and vital organs cried out for some tissue-building protein.

Very few mothers can long endure their children's plea for food, especially when no progress is being made with the near starvation diet I was participating in. Soon she gave in to my pleas and started preparing me foods rich in protein such as poultry, eggs, fish, and some high protein grain cereals. Almost immediately I could feel these foods taking hold of my weakened body, and filling it with the much-needed strength. Unlike the predictions of the doctors concerning such a diet, my body started getting stronger and stronger and my vital organs also began to pick up the endurance and strength that

they needed to carry on my body function.

Throughout my elementary school years and even in junior high, I was a little behind some of the other boys in size and strength, due to my near-fatal illness. All of this time I was gaining on basically high protein foods. I ate many raw eggs, which gave me much strength, and I personally feel that eggs are quite good for us, in spite of the cholesterol jag we seem to be on.

As my high school days rolled around, I became very interested in athletics, and by that time I was actually larger than most my age, and quite a bit stronger. I was certainly destined to be a good athlete, and I feel basically this was because of my high protein diet, which saved me from being the proverbial ninety-seven pound weakling.

On many occasions I can remember, instead of taking my extra spending money and buying sweets, I would buy various types of canned fish that my body seemed to constantly crave. Most of my attention in high school turned toward eating meat (beef and lamb) that was quite rare. Heretofore I had always preferred meat that was well done, even to the point of almost being charred. This is actually the way my family had always prepared meat dishes, and my taste naturally developed in this way. I found that not only did the meat taste better rare, but it seemed to digest faster and give me more strength.

In college, I first started lifting weights and I even put more emphasis on my diet after I began to do this weight training. As weeks passed I took my weight training more seriously, and certainly my diet. It seems that even though the college dining table offered a variety of good foods, these foods were a little dead as far as nutrition was concerned. Certainly the meat and vegetables were cooked too thoroughly for the body to break down the digestible protein and vitamin content. I felt if I was going to really be a competitive weightlifter I must choose my own diet and have a proper gym to train in, so I gave up college for a career in weight training.

On returning to my home, and the reluctant consent of my parents to allow me to postpone my college career for a while, I was able to study nutrition and develop my eating habits along even more productive lines. I knew basically that I needed a great quantity of protein to build and repair the muscle tissue I was tearing down with the heavy lifting. It made sense to me that the more protein my body could assimilate, the greater progress I could make in my quest for weightlifting championships.

Although throughout my high school and college years, I was a very large and active athlete, I never had a tremendous appetite. This was somewhat of a handicap, since I needed to eat more digestible protein to enable my heavy training program to be successful. As I examined the situation, I came to the conclusion that even though I could not eat a great deal of solid foods, I always consumed large quantities of liquids. Much of my diet had been made up of milk, from which I received much good digestible protein. Throughout my junior high and high school years, I had sometimes consumed three to four quarts of milk per day. Now part of the task before me was to figure out a way to put protein in a drinkable form.

My first pursuit of a higher protein diet, in a liquid form, was to go back on the raw eggs and sweet milk. By beating them up in a blender, I could drink about a dozen eggs at a time, which would give me much extra protein along with the milk. I found that this once again enhanced my ability to gain weight and to build strong healthy muscle tissue, after it had been torn down before in my workout.

It doesn't take very long for anyone to get a little fed up on just one diet. Naturally the same routine day after day, of raw eggs, even though it was taken along with an otherwise well-balanced diet, made me grow to the point where I grossly disliked milk with raw eggs.

Now I had gone just as far as my heretofore education of diet had allowed me, so I had to learn other protein foods that I could mix in liquid form. At this time the various soybean supplements had not been presented on most markets, and even those who were quite experienced in nutrition and so-called proper diets, were just now beginning to realize that the "strength athlete" needed something more than just a diet made up of regular high protein foods. I read somewhere that soybean powder was very good for protein deficiency, and it was being shipped overseas for starving people in various parts of the world. I thought surely if this was good for someone with a gross lack of protein, it would be extra nourishing for a person that needed more protein because of his strenuous exercise. Finally I was able to buy some soybean meal. This product was quite course in comparison with the finely crushed power we know in the protein supplements today. Although it was in this crude manner, I was able to grind it a bit finer by beating it in a milk solution for a long period of time with the aid of a blender. I could immediately tell the difference in my diet and thought actually that the two protein supplements I had tried thus far, both being good, should be combined in some way, which would give me the better quantities of both. I started varying my diet, making ice cream and milk shakes with the soybean meal, raw eggs, milk, and varying the type of flavor used. Even better results were obtained from this particular procedure.

My search went on for more protein foods that could be used in a concentrated form and taken in liquids. One day I was reading the label on a plain gelatin product, and saw that they boasted it to be very high in protein. I thought this would be something to try so I started putting it into orange juice, stirring it up briskly and drinking it. This I used along with the diet of milk, raw eggs, and soybeans. Now there was a greater vitality in my

life, and certainly a marked difference in my training. I varied the gelatin products, many being on the market, and started buying it in a bulk form. Now I started to learn that both animal and vegetable proteins were better when they were used together.

This value of using animal and vegetable protein in a blend proved itself more as time went by. I kept up my search for new types of protein supplement, and one day being in a small Georgia town, went by a peanut mill. I asked them what they did with the by-product of peanut oil they were famous for. They said it was turned into cattle feed and was much sought after because of its high protein quality. I'd always been a lover of peanuts prepared in various ways, and was sure that if I could find some of this by-product in an edible form it would be profitable to my training. This was accomplished and with the help of my Dad, we set up a tiny electrical mill to pulverize the caked dry mass that was left after the peanut oil was extracted. I mixed this with my soybean meal, and used it as a permanent part of my diet.

There is no doubt in my mind that the secret to success in any sport is diet along with rest and exercise, and of course the proper mental attitude. As I grew in size and my lifting progressed to world record breaking performances, I knew that one secret to my success was the ability to train more than anyone else. I could actually train on the same lift every day. I believe the secret to this is furnishing the body with enough digestible protein to allow the muscle tissue to rebuild quite rapidly. The more I learned of nutrition the faster my strength went up, and the more I was able to train. I also learned that my body needed all types of protein, but it could develop better on the animal variety. Not that I had any desire to omit the valuable protein coming from vegetables, but I feel that I should pursue other forms of animal protein.

I remember that during the time I started really making progress in my convalescence, from the illness as a small boy, my mother not only gave me the meat, milk, fish and eggs prepared in various ways, but she also prepared various strength-building soups for me. This soup was usually made up of some canned variety in which she added a liquid that she squeezed with a hand press from ground beef. She would put the beef on the stove in a large pan and add some water. As this started to get hot she would allow it to simmer for about a minute, actually just long enough for it to get hot, and then pour it through a lemon squeezing press, that would extract all of the fluid. She would pour this fluid into the soup and serve it to me in that manner. Thinking of this, I decided I would add this type of strength-builder to my then fortified protein diet, and every morning for breakfast this is what I would have to start my strenuous day. With these great quantities of protein, I found that my body was growing a little stale, even though I ate many green vegetables and salads, and tried to have what I would call a well-balanced diet of various vegetables both cooked and raw. Occasionally I would drink soft drinks during my training and noticed when I did this I could perform much better, and my digestive cycle would work much faster. This proved to me that I needed a great deal more sugar. It seemed that the more protein I took, the more sugar I needed to help digest the protein, and also give me quick energy. I turned to the greatest sugar supply that I could find, which was honey. I soon found that much of the honey that could be bought in grocery stores did not do me as much good as honey direct from the beehive, bought from some farmer. It was my personal belief that much of the honey that was on the market had been heated in a pasteurizing process and had lost some of its quick digesting qualities.

Some days I would consume even a half pint of honey, when I

was working out strenuously and carrying on my tremendous traveling schedule.

Now having learned of my body's need for extra sugar, to go along with the great amounts of protein I was taking in, I even did better with my training and actual performances.

Naturally, my performances of breaking world records, winning championships, and even the Olympic games proved that my ideas on protein food are successful along with my training, rest, and mental attitudes.

I think basically, as I discuss in the next chapter, the main thing that an athlete needs to become great, is the will. Naturally everyone has different potentials, but the person who will endure almost any discomfort to achieve his ultimate potential is the one who is going to achieve championships caliber. I know this previous statement is a very obvious one and one that will be sanctioned by all those who will read this publication. But I especially at this time speak of diet. Many of the foods I eventually included in my diet, foods that have proven their valuable qualities, are quite distasteful to the average person. I've had people to look at some of the things that I was eating, and especially after I told them the contents, would turn up their noses and say, "I would not eat anything like that!" My answer has always been, "It depends on how much you want to be a champion!"

I guess the first distasteful food I started to use was the extract from raw beef. I have always been very careful about the beef I chose for such a dish, since I was eating it without any type of cooking. The procedure here is to take good ground beef, of the lean variety and put it in one of the better centrifugal force liquid extractors. This will extract most of the liquid, which looks mostly like blood. I usually add a little salt to this liquid, and drink it. Considering all of the liquid supplements I have used, this is one of the greatest. This meat extract can be disguised by drinking it in tomato juice, or adding some type of meat sauce to it to change the flavor. I expanded this through the years, and not only used beef, but all types of raw seafoods. With a diet of all the protein supplements that I have mentioned, and also using the raw beef extracts and raw seafoods, whether liquefied or used in a solid form, I found that I could put in some eighteen hours a day in my traveling and speaking engagements, plus carry on a workout routine.

I have experimented with many other types of extra protein foods, some I can half-heartedly recommend and some that I condemn completely. I tried one time to drink pure beef blood. This food, that many of the old-time strong men used, is quite hard to secure, but I found one meat-packing house that would furnish it for me. Especially in this procedure, one has to have a person that he can trust to secure the blood, and of course to secure it in a sanitary manner, and then be quite discreet in what type animal the blood is taken from. To keep the blood from coagulating, I found that a little citric acid mixed with water, previously placed in the container, would do the trick.

Concerning this diet of beef blood, I never found it as rewarding, in a strength-building sense as the beef extracts. I believe that from the extracts not only blood is obtained, but also other fluids and meat tissue that are also valuable.

Along with all of these foods that I recommend, I have always used a vitamin mineral supplement, and on most occasions taken large quantities of cold-pressed wheat germ oil.

Naturally each individual has to feel out his own personal needs, which are basically the same in all of us. All of the protein supplements that I have told about here should naturally not be taken all at one time, but should be alternated, first using one and then the other. Some of them may not wholly agree with many people, but as I said, basically we are all the

same and have the same needs. I cannot say exactly that all I have done to gain my strength, through diet, will be good for everyone, but I am just telling you what has been the key to my personal success.

Many of the foods that I have named will come as no revelation to many, but I believe that most will agree my pioneering in the world of diet has turned up many thoughts and ideas concerning body-building foods.

I have purposely not dealt in technical terms in presenting these foods to you. I feel my readers will be of many different origins and various educational backgrounds, so I have told these things in plain layman's language.

Diet cannot do it alone. There are many qualities that make up the champion athlete, or just the person who wants to live the full and vibrant life, getting the most use out of what God has given him. Certainly all will agree, the type of fuel we put into the wonderful machines we call bodies is what makes it operate, either efficiently or in a half-hearted way.

Chapter 3

BENCH PRESSING

While bench pressing, a man is first assumed to be resting completely on a horizontal support, giving all of his faith and trust to that support as he lowers the bar from arm length to the chest, observes a pause and once again pushes it back to arms length. During this movement the successful bench presser is indeed not giving all of his faith and confidence in the horizontal support, but is in a chosen stance, being far from relaxed.

Each individual, staying within the rules of course, should choose his own stance for the bench press. The body being flat on the surface of the bench is the first consideration, then with the feet pulled back under the lifter and spread wide enough to be comfortable, but also to give each side of the body efficient support. I personally choose to pull my feet back under me as far as possible, and still allow them to stay flat on the floor. (Figure 1)

The next move to insure a good bench-pressing stance is to try to pull the shoulders toward the hips, in more or less an arching of the back movement. By getting in this position, making sure that no part of the body is illegally raised from the bench, you are coiled for action. (also in Figure 1) The athlete is not mercilessly wallowing on his support, but is ready to not only lift

Figure 1

the weight in the proper manner, but prepared to overcome any misbalancing effect that may occur while the attempt is being carried out.

If you are a beginner, make sure that you start off with a good bench-pressing stance; or on the other hand, if you are a seasoned veteran and feel that you have fallen into a bad position on the bench, reexamine your stance and correct it for maximum effectiveness in the lift.

Just as important as the stance on the bench is the width of a lifter's grip on the bar. The rules governing the movement provide that the athlete can have his hands 32 inches apart. This means that one would want to adjust his grip from the beginning of the knurling, at the center of the bar, to the maximum width allowed. The 32 inches given seems to be a fair figure for everyone, or at least I have never heard any complaints about it. Before this rule was made by the Amateur Athletic Union, after deciding to sanction power lifting meets and keep records on the same, many lifters used a collar to collar grip, and by bouncing the weight on the chest could handle a great poundage. Naturally the wider the grip, the poorer the start for the chest and stronger finish the lifter has.

I had the privilege of being present when the power lifting rules were being discussed at an A.A.U. convention. I attended to ask for my reinstatement as an amateur, and since I was already there, the committee set up to establish the governing regulations for power lifting, asked me to sit in. During this first session I suggested 32 inches for the maximum allowed width of the hands for the bench press. My way of thinking was that if there was going to be a pause at the chest, this was just about as wide a grip as could be successfully used by the lifter if a good start was going to be achieved. My suggestion came only after the collar-to-collar grip was completely ruled out, and a mandatory pause at the chest was made a regulation.

The way the individual athlete is built has much to do with the grip he should choose for the maximum poundage. The wider the grip the more pectoral muscles are used, and as the hand spacing comes in, more of the deltoid and triceps muscle groups are called on to perform. Thus, it is imperative for each individual to experiment with grip spacing and decide the best for his use.

Never decide that one particular hand spacing is forever. Not only should the beginner find a hand spacing that is more suitable for his build, but also the veteran lifter should occasionally experiment to see if his development has altered any through constant exercises. One may be surprised to see that after months or even years of training some muscle groups have developed faster than others, so a difference in hand spacing could be an advantage.

Whether a person uses a regular thumbs around the bar, or thumbs out position can also be experimented with and a decision made. This too can altar as time goes by, so don't ever be afraid to experiment a little here. One more consideration is just where should the bar touch on the chest at the bottom position. This decision must also be made by the athlete himself. Most feel that the highest point of the chest is the best, but I have always said that wherever the "groove" allows the bar to rest is preferable for a particular lifter. Wherever the natural striking point comes is usually where the bar should remain for the pause at the chest. There are several things that one could consider in getting his bench press into the "groove." First, as a rule, the bar is going to travel not only upward but a little backward over the upper part of the chest or lower neck as it proceeds to the lockout position. (Figure 2) This is the natural traveling path of the

Figure 2

bar, and should be considered as it is driven off the chest. Many maximum lifts are lost when the first thrust allows the bar to travel downward toward the belt line instead of in the natural "groove." When the bar goes this way the leverage begins to work against the athlete.

ROUTINES

All of these routines I have tried and at one time or the other found them to be very productive. Just how long any lifter stays on one particular routine for one lift must be left strictly up to him. As many of you know, I have always liked to work out every day, using what is commonly known as the split routine. In my power lifting I have usually done bench presses and the assistance exercises for that lift on one day and squats and dead lifts and the exercises that help them along on the next. Usually taking a day's layoff after four straight days of workouts.

Sets in a routine must be left up to the individual. My recommendation is to start out with one set after warming up properly and then continuing on as the muscles respond and become toned to as many sets as one feels is necessary. One type of personal education that can only be self-taught is when to change from one routine to the other. A lifter should never wait until he goes stale to change routines in a particular endeavor, but learn his body well enough to know when this staleness is approaching and change before his lift stops escalating. Learn yourself well, and then you will know when to change to other assistance exercises for the bench press or in fact any lift you are trying to strengthen.

ROUTINE I

Let's start out with one of my all-time favorite bench press routines, which is very simple but has always been effective. The first of as many sets as you would like to include starts with a warm-up at the bench press and an extra barbell at the foot of your bench. After the warm-up do one set of 8's in the regular bench press and then immediately turn around on your bench completely reverse from the barbell used for the lift. At this time I like to do heavy breathing along with bent arm pullovers using this extra barbell originally placed at the foot of the bench. Have this weight relatively light; let's say something that you could easily do 20 repetitions with. Immediately after you have replaced your bench press in the rack or allowed your spotters to remove it, make your turn on the bench and do a set of 10's with the light barbell in the bent arm pullover movement. While doing this exercise take in just as much breath as you possibly can as you approach the low position, and exhale after pulling the weight overhead toward the chest. (Figures 3 & 4)

The eight bench presses and ten bent-arm pullovers we will call one set. Repeat this for as many sets as you would like. I usually do about five while using this as my bench press routine. The purpose and results of the bent arm pullovers are several. One is to, of course, work the muscle groups

Figure 3

Figure 4

that you are using for bench presses. Another is that this is a great rib cage expander, and by doing the heavy breathing when the weight is pulling tremendously at the upper body the rib cage can be expanded, making for a larger chest and more development. By using a lighter weight you should find that while doing this movement you are not only accomplishing the latter, but you are also recovering from the set of 8's on the bench press.

ROUTINE II

This is also one of my favorites and has given great results through the years, and as you will notice like all the others, it always includes some type of the exercises which we are endeavoring to enhance. I developed a theory years ago that is quite simple and has always proven true. That is, "When doing an assistance exercise to increase a particular lift, always include that lift in the routine." The reason for this is to continue to coordinate the strength that is being built by the assistance exercises into the lift that is really being concentrated on.

On Routine II warm up and do one set of heavy bench presses for about three reps. Immediately after the exercise do a set of hand stand presses, ranging from 10 to 15. (It all depends on just how many you can do.) I realize that it can be quite confusing to just say "hand stand presses" because there could be so many variations of this movement. Allow me at this time to explain what I would like. I have always tried to do these movements in more of a cheating fashion. By putting my feet against the wall, (Figures 5 and 6) and going through the movement, you can see that my upper body is quite a bit away from the wall itself, allowing me to go into a semi-dip on the bench pressing movement. The purpose of this exercise is to carry out the theory that I have been preaching for years, that is "Reverse Blood Flow Method." Immediately after the hand stand presses I have always liked to go back to the bench press for a set of 10's. This will cause some weight changes on the bar, some of the heavier weight you originally did the three reps with will have to be removed. The three exercises: bench press, set of 3's, hand stand presses (maximum up to 15), and the 10 bench presses will constitute a complete set. Do as many as you feel will help you, always remembering to start off conservatively. When working on this routine I usually do five sets.

Figure 5

Figure 6

ROUTINE III

Here is one that you probably haven't tried. Warm up and do ten bench presses with a weight that works you pretty well. Then with the assistance of a couple of friends take a heavy dumbbell in one hand while you are in the prone position on the bench. You must distort this position a little by moving to one side so that you can grasp one of the uprights that hold the weights with the hand not holding the dumbbell. With you secure in this position, lower the dumbbell into an extreme one-arm bench press position and raise it up again. (Figures 7 and 8) When doing this try to almost perform what once was called the "flying exercise" as done with two dumbbells. By using only one dumbbell and the other hand as a support and really a helper you can perform this in a cheating manner and handle a great weight. This goes back to one of my original theories of handling the most weight on every muscle that is possible. You can handle more weight with the one dumbbell than if you had two. Use this movement for about five reps with each arm. The more you do it the more weight that you can handle even without gaining more strength, because you will gain a little bit more form and more know-how in cheating on it. This will give the one side being worked a tremendous amount of strength, or anyway it has done so for me.

Figure 7

Figure 8

About three sets is what I have found works out best. A set constituted of ten bench presses and five one-arm dumbbell bench presses with each hand.

ROUTINE IV

Since we are talking about the dumbbell on the bench, let's consider a routine on occasions of just dumbbells. Here we are not deviating from the theory of always doing the exercises that the assistance movements are designed to enhance, because we are doing the bench press movement only with the hands turned the other way and with a little longer movement. I point out it being a little longer movement because the dumbbells will drop lower than a barbell which is restricted by the touching of your chest. On this routine let's use the heavy and light system, that actually we use on almost everything that we do. Warm up with a light pair of dumbbells then do five reps with heavy ones handed to you by your partners and then go back to the lighter ones for about twenty reps. I recommend three sets of these. Once again repeating, five reps with the heavy dumbbells followed by twenty reps with the lighter ones, which makes up one set. (Figures 9 and 10)

Figure 9 (above), Figure 10 (below)

ROUTINE V

The fifth and last routine I will give you is a real killer. I have waited until last because you must be in tremendous condition to do this particular routine. It has to do with the theory of lowering a heavy weight with as much resistance as possible. I will first describe how I like to do the exercise, and then talk about the "whys." A set is as follows: warm up and do one set of 10's with a weight that works you, then with two strong spotters have the weight loaded to at least a hundred pounds more than your top bench press. It all depends on just how the movement goes, deciding on how much more weight to put on than you can bench press. You will have to experiment with this before deciding on a poundage.

Have your spotters take the weight off the rack and hand it to you in a good up position. Then begin to lower the weight to your chest. As you begin your lowering movement have the spotters to continue holding to each end of the bar so that they can stop the weight along with their other responsibility. The other responsibility is the main one, and that is to bear their weight evenly on the bar mashing down on your resistance steadily. As you pass through a strong point they will have to press a little harder and in the weak points let up a little bit. The object is not for you to control the weight as it comes down, but to actually be fighting with all your strength at all times as it is pushed down on you. With the weight loaded heavier than you can bench press your spotters will not have to push down so hard with their own weight, and will have better control of what they are doing. As soon as the weight touches the chest the spotters should release it and allow you to push back up on it as much as possible. Each time when reaching the sticking point once again lowering it back to the chest. Do about three reps while it is down. At

that time let the spotters once again get their grip on the bar and lift it back to arm's length. Repeating their first assignment, pressing the weight back down to your chest. At that time you are to do three more heavy raises off of the chest and turn it back over to them. Three good reps like this is about all that a man in tremendous condition can stand.

Now for the "whys." I know that throughout the years the theory of lowering the weight has been tried and on many occasions discarded. The discarding of the theory has usually been because a person has only done one rep and then had to get out from under the weight and put it back up or he has had to have it lifted off. In this matter we are doing reps, which I have found to be quite productive. Also in the past many have become discouraged with the lowering movement because they lowered a weight that they had under control and were giving into the weight to allow it to come down. Even a weight that they could not bench press could be lowered under such control. What I am telling you to do is to fight with all of your might while this weight is being forced on you by the spotters. (Figure 11)

Of course the three reps of pushing it off the chest is to give a great deal of starting power for your regular bench press. I recommend about three sets on this lift, or as you find that you personally should do. A set being ten reps on the bench press and three or as you would like on the heavy lowering movement.

Figure 11

Have your spotters practice with you on a lighter weight before attempting the real heavy ones. By doing this they can get themselves coordinated.

Here I have given you five of the greatest routines that I have ever worked up. Some of them you have possibly done before, or at least variations of them. Others may be new to you. I would personally think that it would take about a year to go through all of them, and you may use each of them for the period of time that you think is necessary. As I have said before, everyone is an individual and one of the main things you should know is when you are about to go stale and should switch from one of these routines to the other.

Chapter 4

DEEP KNEE BEND

I am sure by now that everyone understands my theories on the deep knee bend so I will not go into it further other than to just talk about how, and maybe throw in a why here, there, and the other.

First, we must be as comfortable as possible in all lifts and especially in the deep knee bend. There are so many different sizes and shapes of people with so many different makeups that it is hard to say what is just right for everyone. Basically, we are going to have to do a deep knee bend in a manner that puts the weight squarely on the thigh muscles, which means keeping a straight back. Any time that we lean forward on the recovery of a deep knee bend more than just to keep our balance, we are distorting the lifting and in turn not doing it properly. To add to this we are cheating ourselves out of much strength that could be placed in the legs by putting it off on other muscle groups. Considering all of this let's try to do a deep knee bend with a straight back and go down into the low position, rising again in the same way.

(Left to right, Figures 12 and 13)

To accomplish having a straight back squat, some lifters must of course put their heels on a board so that they will not be in a strain in this position. The bar placed across the shoulders and back of the neck is never going to be the most comfortable thing going, so in practicing, a pad should be used and only the "limit tries" should be used with a bare bar. I feel that sometime in the future the bar for a contest will have to be larger than our regular 1 1/16 inch bars, because these are going to be quite dangerous with 900 plus poundages.

Try to squat naturally. By this, I mean to try to make it a natural movement. Judge your foot spacing and heel height to what feels good to you. Don't try to get in an unnatural position just to handle more weight. In the long run this is going to work down on your poundage instead of build it up as you may temporarily think.

The rules say that the top of the thigh must be parallel to the floor to make for a full squat. Many have cheated themselves by just shooting for this parallel position and stopping before they go all the way down. I make this statement because I think much power can be built in a real low position to help drive all the way up through the "sticking point." The only reason I would tell a lifter never to go all the way to the bottom in a full squat is if it gave him tremendous back pains and soreness. I am not talking about just temporary soreness, but a chronic ailment in this area. If a temporary soreness occurs just from stretching the body into the deep knee bend position, and then goes away after a few other workouts I will stick to my original recommendation. Go all the way down.

ROUTINE I

The first routine that I am going to recommend will be scoffed at by some and overlooked by others as they seek a more intricate exercise session, but I urge you to include this in your workout whether you are a beginner or veteran lifter. I think that through the years I have overcome more stale periods by doing three sets of 10's than any other remedy for overwork with heavier weights and various assistance exercises. Considering this I will ask you to do a routine of three sets of ten reps after a warm-up. As always, judge your own resting period between sets. If you are not in condition to do three sets of 10's, you may start off with one and work up to ten. I say this because not only is this a good routine to overcome a feeling of staleness but it is good for coming back after a layoff, as well as for the beginner. It gets you into the "groove" as well as builds size and strength.

ROUTINE II

This second routine is going to sound elementary because I am going to ask you to go from the three sets of 10's to three sets of 3's. A greater warm-up will be necessary because I want you to do three sets of 3's with the weight that you feel is appropriate, and will work you properly. The three sets of 3's will take some of the size and expansion that has been put into the muscle from your three sets of 10's and will add some real strength to your squatting power. You will have to be very careful on your sets of 3's that you do not go "stale." For so many times you will find this happening after gaining strength from the movements when doing them for several workouts. At this point you are going to possibly feel that I am not being consistent in my instructions, for the bench press routines I gave were recommended for any sequence and

times that you desired, just so one at a time was used. Now you are finding that I am recommending one squatting routine to follow the other. I am quite conscious of this, and the reason is very simple. I am writing from experience and not on theory. These squatting routines can be used at any time, but I am bringing you straight through them at least once, because I want you to approach the last one in good condition. Like all the other routines, you may later use them at your pleasure.

ROUTINE III

There comes a time in any squatting routine that progress is going to slow down unless a quarter squatting system is brought in. (Figures 14 and 15) I realize that many of you have done all variations of the squat, but after doing the three sets of 3's, I recommend bringing the quarter squat into your routine in this manner. Warm up, do a set of 10's, and then a set of five reps in the quarter squat. These two movements will constitute a set and at this point in your workout as I have recommended, you should be able to do at least three sets consisting of these two movements.

One of the key words in quarter squatting is safety. Handling a weight that you can only raise about four to six inches can be quite dangerous

Figure 14

Figure 15

if safety precautions are not taken. This can be handled in many ways and here are a few that I have used.

The first is the use of a power rack as we have grown to know it in the past few years. This consists of two upright supports on each side with the bar traveling in between. At graduated intervals, a pin is put through the uprights to rest the weight on. This is a safe way of performing the movement. That is, raising the weight off of the pin from the quarter squat position up into an upright stance. Another I have used, which is also foolproof as far as falling with the weight or pushing the weight off of the stands, is to actually weld legs onto a bar. Two widely spaced legs on each side secured permanently to the bar, allowing the weights to be put on either end, is one of the most desired methods. Of course, it has to be made just for the height of the one person using it. Picture it as being something like a modified version of a carpenter's sawhorse. I have found that using a quarter squat bar and racks is most ideal. It consists of two heavy squat racks with a permanent loop over each end so that the bar cannot get out. The racks are equipped with automobile bumper jacks so that they can be raised and lowered to the desired position. I realize that others are using these, but I believe that I had them in operation several years before I saw anyone else employing the idea.

By no means try to do the quarter squat under conditions where the bar is free, for it will surely invite accidents, sometimes very serious ones.

ROUTINE IV

In this routine we will keep the quarter squat and arrange it in a position that I feel is most advantageous in an advanced program. First do ten reps in the full squat after a proper warm-up. Then three quarter squats with a weight that is quite adequate for that amount of reps. Next, do three full squats with a weight that works you quite well and then round out the set with one-legged squats. (Figure 16)

Figure 16

One-legged squats can be performed in many ways with many degrees of results. I personally have found the best way to accomplish these is to do them by standing with the leg to be worked on a bench or low table that will allow the athlete to go down into a full knee bend position on the one leg and rise again without the other leg touching the floor. To better explain, the leg not in use is to hang off the edge of the bench or table as the exercise is being performed. Do as many of these with each leg as possible, working up to about twenty reps. If balance is a problem, there is no harm in placing a hand or finger against the wall or a near object to keep balance, just as long as it is not used to help the lift itself.

Again, three sets of this routine are preferred. A set consists of ten squats, three quarter squats, three full squats, and as many one-legged squats as possible, working up to about twenty.

ROUTINE V

At this time I would like for you to consider an exercise that I have found to be quite productive along with my squatting routines, and I have read that some of the European Olympic lifters have discovered that jumping movements have also been good for them. This is exactly what I am talking about: jumping. When our weightlifting team was traveling for the State Department in 1955, I remember I would get some real strange looks and sometimes many questions when I would go leaping around the warm-up room or stadium grounds in what we would call jump-squat movements. In performing this, I would go all the way down into a full squat position and leap forward and as high as possible. By exerting as much leaping power as possible, much strain is put on the muscles, and in turn, the groups being exercised are stimulated and strengthened just as though a slower movement was being done with weights.

Figure 17

Figure 18

Figure 19

As years have gone by I have found that the best way to perform this type movement is to leap up on a table. Just like different poundages are handled by different lifters, a different height table is required for those with various abilities to leap flat-footed with a single leap landing flat-footed on the table. (Figures 17, 18, and 19) Make sure that the object that you are leaping up on is fixed so that it cannot slide when it is receiving your total weight. Do these leaping movements in sets of 10's. Leap onto the table, descend to the

floor, and leap again until ten have been accomplished. I believe that you will find this a new and strange sensation in your regular work at this point, making for a different stimulation to the muscles and continuing them on their way to personal records in the squat for you. To incorporate the jumps into a set, do ten going down about halfway into a squatting position for your leaps, five in the regular deep knee bend and five in the quarter squat. These three movements will constitute a set, and work up to three sets.

If, as time goes by, your leaping power increases, surely it is wise to make your table a little higher, to compensate for your new explosive power.

ROUTINE VI

Here we are once again around to the "killer," but this time in the squat. Because we are going to use the down movement, let's eliminate the quarter squat this time, and just use a warm-up in the full squat, and then move to the force down squatting movement. It is more difficult to perform this exercise than it was in the bench press for many reasons. One is that the entire body is involved in doing squats, or almost the entire body. Because of this, the bar must be forced down by the spotters in a straight movement. If one spotter pushes too fast or not fast enough, injuries could occur to the athlete. Like the instructions in the bench press, the lifter must always have a set of spotters who are strong enough to adequately handle the weight used, if called on to do so. You and the spotters must coordinate yourselves together to bring the weight down evenly. Practice a little with lighter weights before going to something that will actually do the work. To do the down lift in the squatting position, load the bar heavier than the natural squat, or more than you can do in one rep in the natural deep knee bend, and allow the spotters to help you lift the bar from the rack and assist you as you step back into the squatting position. Variations of this can be worked out on a power rack by removing the pins when the bar is brought up and then the spotters help to force the weight down, or other safety devices can be used such as parallel bars at the squat position, weights large enough to hit the floor when the athlete can't back up, etc. The latter is the reason that I have used the large wheels for my deep knee bends in training for years. Many people have been impressed with these tremendous wheels that weight about 400 pounds apiece, but the real purpose of them has been just to touch the floor if I have added more weight to the bar than I can get up with. This helps as a safety factor such as the others I have named.

To continue our instructions on actually performing: as the spotters back up with the lifter, they should help him get in position and then when ready, the lifter should start down himself naturally in the lift. Many lifters would have ten times strength enough to hold all the poundage the spotters could place on the bar, if the knees were not voluntarily broken. After the knees are slightly bent and the bar is being brought down, the spotters are in control of how much weight they are putting on the bar as they have their hands in the position where they can either lift or push down. (Figure 20) If this weight is adequate to work the higher position in the squat, which is not as necessary as the sticking point in low position, the spotters will have to be quite careful that they allow the bars to slow down as the sticking point and lower positions are reached. Of course, working the high side of the squat is not as important since we are doing so many quarter squats. The main thing we want to

Figure 20

consider is the sticking point and low position as the lifter fights the weight, when the spotters are pressing it down. When the bottom is reached, the lifter should do just about the same movement as he did in the bench press. That is, try to drive up from the low position three times. Coming up as high into the sticking point as he possibly can, and fighting it, and going down to the bottom and attempting it two more times. After this, the spotters can pull the weight back up to standing position, and they will probably have to handle most of this weight, because the lifter is going to be pretty well exhausted after his three attempts on the bottom. Pushing him down two more times with each bottom position being a foundation for the three upper tries again, these spotters then should help the athlete up for the last time and carefully place the bar back on the racks. As I have said, power racks are very good for this movement to be performed in, since the lifter doesn't have to take a step backward or forward from the racks before doing his lifts. In performing a set of this particular routine, which consists of ten repetitions in the deep knee bend and the three downward movements with each containing three attempts to rise before the spotters help the lifter up, the athlete must decide exactly how to modify the routine for his particular use. If at the start one force down knee bend with the lifter fighting as hard as possible against the spotters and then doing the three upward attempts at the bottom before being lifted up again exhaust him, he should call it a day without doing the other two repetitions. If two seems to be adequate, that should be what is included. Anyway, how many repetitions you choose to do in the down position is up to you, but I would recommend working up to three even though you cannot do but one set consisting of the ten deep knee bends and three force down movements. Three sets should be the limit.

ROUTINE VII

This particular routine is one that you have read in strength magazines or in one of my previous courses, if you have followed lifting for awhile. I do not claim it being new with me, but I do feel that I have done more experimenting with it than anyone else, and in turn, have written more than any other instructor. My personal name for it is Progressive Movement Training. This is the only time I am going to ask you to deviate from my rule of thumb of always doing the actual movement, because I feel with all the reps you have been doing in the deep knee bends, you are pretty well in the groove and will not get out in the time that you spend on the Progressive Movement squatting routine.

The real trick to doing the Progressive Movement Routine is repetitions as well as lengthening the movement. For those who have not read any of my instructions on this routine before, let me explain it thoroughly. The idea of doing this in the squat is to start off with a quarter squat lift in a power rack situation, or a squat rack with some type of guards running up each side to keep the weight from falling out in case of a loss of balance. If you would like to just makeshift something for this, you could run two bards, pipes, 2 x 4's, etc. up each set of squat racks and tape or wire them on temporarily. The sturdier you can make such an apparatus, the better. If you have access to power racks, then your problem is solved without modification.

By starting off in a quarter squat, you should use a weight about 100 pounds more than your best full squat. I realize this is a very light weight in comparison to what you can quarter squat with, but this is part of the plan. I recommend doing about twenty to twenty-five repetitions in this quarter squatting movement with the particular weight that fits your ability, performing two sets. The twenty to twenty-five repetitions will constitute

a set. I want you to do this every day. After doing the two sets, you are going to feel, especially in the beginning, that you are not accomplishing very much so you will not be very tired. Every three days, lower the weight or raise the body, which will come out to the same results, about three inches. When lowering the weight three inches, knock off three reps. Continue the two sets of eighteen or twenty reps, according to what you started with, for three days, then raise the body or lower the stands again some three inches, knocking off three to four repetitions in each set. Continue doing this until you have worked just as far down as you possibly can into a full squatting position; always starting the lift at the low position of the bar. After you have worked down just as far as possible cutting your repetitions all the way down to two, rest about two to three days and then try your limit in the squat. I believe that you will find that you have gained quite a bit of strength during this drawn out Progressive Movement routine. While you are doing this Progressive Movement routine, you can do your upper body and back exercises as usual, if you feel you can perform all of them.

Much of your recovery ability and your strength progression is up to you as an individual. I am giving you routines that I feel are the ultimate in power building, and many of them quite unique. Much thought and experimentation has gone into these, but one thing that I have learned through experimenting with other athletes and on myself is that each and every one is an individual. You must learn to judge your repetitions, and especially your sets according to your personal ability and responsiveness to the exercises themselves.

Another tip on doing this Progressive Movement routine is to use one-inch sheets of plyboard for your graduation. If you will cut these one-inch sheets of plyboard just square enough for your stance in the squat allowing safety foot room on each side, you can stack them up as you lengthen the movement. I have given some ideas on squat racks for this including the power rack's use, but you may even go as far as I have in the movement, if finances will allow. I use the heavy quarter squat racks with bumper jacks built in, (Figures 14 and 15) and I can just lower and raise them at will. If you cannot afford to build such equipment, or if at this time you do not wish to, either power racks will work out adequately for the exercise, or squat racks with extra guards built up each side to extend to a length above your standing position.

I have suggested in the squatting routine that you build on the program of using the routines in sequence, but if you happen to be a very advanced lifter and would like to choose them at random, that is also up to you.

Figure 14

Figure 15

Chapter 5

THE DEAD LIFT

I have spent much time and thought on the dead lift, and the main reason being that I am the world's poorest dead lifter. I believe at the date of this publication, I have actually raised more poundage in the lift than anyone else, but in comparison to some of my other lifts, I am rather ashamed of what I have done. Ashamed possibly is not the word to use, because I have a tremendously bad leverage for the lift, as most large bodied people do. The ideal dead lifter is a person with long limbs and a short body, but no matter how we look at it, we are usually favored or discriminated against in one of the three power lifts, no matter how we are built. This usually evens it all out and makes it relatively fair for everyone. The point I am making is that if you are rather poor in a lift, you do more thinking on it, and consequently come up with better ideas and training methods.

I also must give the credit for some of my knowledge in the dead lift to Bob Peoples. Bob lifted back in the day when power lifting was not a recognized sport, and was quite alone. At 181 pounds or actually less, he raised 725 pounds. Considering everything I know about Bob Peoples and his training conditions, I must say that he is surely the greatest dead lifter that I have ever known.

To dwell just a moment more on philosophy and my friend Bob Peoples, let me say that he has always been one of the greatest thinkers in the weightlifting world. Because of this, I was able to learn various things about the dead lift that would seldom come to most athletes because of my close association with Bob.

From the instructions and philosophy so far, you can see that I am always very sensitive and aware of a lifter's position and procedure in carrying out a lift. I have called the correct manner in each athlete performing the desired movement the "groove," and that is exactly what we are discussing: the particular manner in which each individual finds it easiest to make the lift, always considering of course, performing in a legal manner.

I have observed lifters that looked like they made all their attempts in one motion. To better explain this, personally I have found that whether I am pressing, bench pressing, squatting, etc., I seem to have to change gear as the bar travels through its particular cycles. On the other hand, I have seen fellows who rammed a press to arms length or stood straight up with a dead lift in almost a sudden gesture, without any evidence of this "changing of gears," which could very well mean the changing of the direction of the bar as it traveled to arms length, to upright position, or as you would stand to a finish position in the squat. These thoughts may seem trivial, but every individual must learn himself and know how he is performing the lift. Working out in front of a mirror, or better still, seeing a film or videotape of one's performances can be of great help in finding out just how the bar is traveling, and deciding whether or not this is the proper manner in which you should perform.

These suggestions concerning the "groove" are important, and this is one of the reasons I have recommended ten repetitions in some of the lifts as we went through other routines. Doing the higher repetitions not only helps pump a great deal of blood into the muscles, which is part of strengthening them, but also gets you accustomed to allowing the bar along your strongest route. Also this is why I say that a lift should be practiced along with assistance exercises to strengthen that particular lift. Coordinate the strength that you are building, while keeping the lift in the "groove."

Before going into our first routine for the dead lift, let's consider the fact that we are going to be doing some variations of the dead lift, and in doing so, we will be performing repetitions. Doing repetitions with a bar loaded heavy enough to work the lower back and other muscle groups used in performing the dead lift makes for one big problem. This difficulty is the tenderness of the human hands, resulting in blisters, callouses, torn skin, etc. The hand is naturally going to get tough as it is called on to do any particular work that puts a strain on the surface, but the soreness that results from each workout, as the lifter holds on to a bar for repetitions, usually cannot be overcome by the next workout. This means that the entire muscle groups worked by the dead lift and its variations are going to be at the mercy of the condition of the lifter's hands.

There is an answer to this and it is not original with me, although I have worked out some variations as the years have gone by. The first answer I saw to this problem was developed by Bob Peoples; and as I have said, I will be mentioning him a great deal in this chapter. He had made two hooks to perform repetition (Figure 21) dead lifts with and fastened them on his wrist by wrapping the upper ends with cloth tapes about 2 ½ inches wide. (Figure 22) In this same manner, many have used straps to help secure the bar while

Figure 21

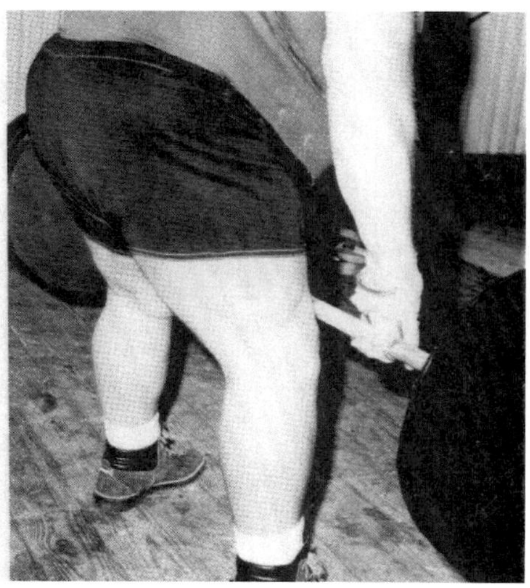

Figure 22

performing repetitions (Figures 23 and 24), but I really believe that the hooks are the best idea. When straps are used, the hands still take a pretty good beating, while they can be far more relaxed when hooks are applied. The hooks have to be made to fit each individual, and can be constructed from any heavy gauge, stiff wire or small rods.

Figure 23

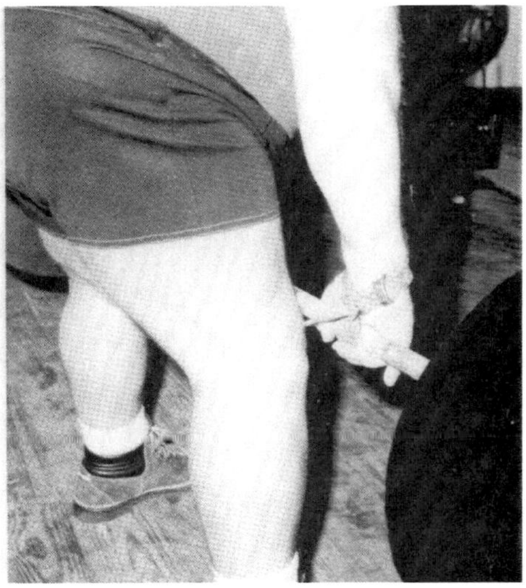

Figure 24

Also before going into routines, let's think about the manner in which the bar is to be gripped. Many reading these instructions will already have their minds made up and through personal experiences know exactly how they would like to grip the bar whether it be concerning the width of hand spacing or manner of holding the bar in the hands. The vast majority of dead lifters I have seen use the reverse grip, securing the bar by hooking the thumbs. The main thing I would like to point out here is that if you use a reverse grip on your heavy singles when attempting a record or in a meet, please also use that same reverse grip when using hooks or straps to do the repetitions. I think much has been lost in the past by lifters who have chosen to go to a straight overhand grip when using these aids in holding the bar, and found that even if they did not recognize it at the time, they were a little handicapped with their reverse grip on the heavy single. I say handicapped referring only to the fact that they were not using the power

that they had developed 100% from repetitions. The simple reason is that the bar was not in the "groove," because of a change in the grip.

To once again put the burden on the individual, allow me to instruct you to lift without the aid of hooks or straps enough so that the hands will be tough and strong when doing heavy singles. This must be left up to you and your own judgment. The aids in gripping are just to allow the back and other muscle groups to be properly worked to gain your ultimate in dead lifting strength.

ROUTINE I

After warming up, the first routine is very simple. Do eight repetitions in regular dead lift lowering the bar all the way to the floor and stopping each time for a new start followed by eight repetitions in the stiff-legged dead lift with the bar just touching the floor and no hesitation each time. (Figures 25 and 26) Eight reps will be the most I will give in dead lifts because breathing is a little difficult while performing the movement. With the bar hanging at arms length and all the weight extending from the shoulders, the rib cage is cramped. A set is eight reps in the regular dead lift and eight in the stiff-legged movement.

Figure 25

Figure 26

ROUTINE II

It is almost imperative to have three bars loaded for this particular routine, or at least have some helpers to make some fast changes if enough weights and bars are not available.

The routine consists of three different lifts and each set should be done in a relatively short period of time. First, after a warm-up, do five repetitions in a regular dead lift. As soon as recovered, do five repetitions in the "top side" of the dead lift, (Figure 27) by raising a bar some four to five inches off parallel racks, boxes, or any other apparatus that you would like to use in raising the bar to a position so that there is only about four to five inches left when lifting the bar to a finish out position. The weight used on this should be something that works the body well for the five reps, and your starting stance should be in the same position that it would have been in if the bar had not been brought from the floor to this point. In other words, I do not want you to get in a real advantage position to handle more weight in this "top side" lift other than the position you would ordinarily have been in had you lifted the bar from the floor. The weight you can handle in this "finish out" should be quite a bit more than in your regular dead lift.

Figure 27

Next, continuing to handle more weight than the regular dead lift, do five repetitions with a bar originating on the floor, and the body in the original starting position for the dead lift. The bar should be loaded to a point

so that it could only be raised about four inches from the floor. (Figure 28)

The two assistance exercises here are naturally to give a good "finish out" and "starting positions" for the dead lift. Many lifters will find that they are extremely strong in one or the other of these positions, but very few will find that they can handle a great deal more weight than their regular lift in both.

Figure 28

No matter what the poundage that can be handled for the five repetitions either in the "top side" or the starting position of the dead lift, load the bar to what you can handle with a good exertion of strength. Work up to three sets in this routine with the regular dead lift, the "top side" movement and the starting movement constituting a set. Five repetitions in each. This is a routine that you may want to come back to occasionally, for it is a very good one. Other routines in the various lifts may work so well that they become favorites and you will want to repeat them every few weeks or months, but also remember that if a routine does not produce now, it very well could later. So try them again.

ROUTINE III

For an assistance exercise on this particular routine let's use the "good morning" exercise. I realize that there are several things that will pop up as objections to the "good morning" lift, but let's do it in a little different manner than usual.

The first time I tried the "good morning" exercise as a strengthening lift for my lower back, I was very satisfied. I started out with a weight that I considered to be ridiculously light, for I wanted to do some high repetitions and also knew that sometimes discomfort resulted from a heavy bar resting in this position. I did these lifts just as strictly as I thought was possible for quite a while and certainly did receive great results from it. The results that I am speaking of came basically from my pulling power in the regular dead lift and also the clean and snatch.

Overly delighted with this particular assistance exercise, I continued doing it and even found I was getting much, much stronger in it, but then my progress in the lifts that I was actually performing this assistance exercise to increase stopped advancing. My first reaction was to consider what was wrong and give it some serious thought. I was not going stale because I was getting stronger in the "good morning" exercise so there must be something else wrong. On real close examination, I found that even though I was continuing to perform the lift with stiff knees, and bending the trunk of the body at least into a parallel position to the floor before rising again, there was indeed something different. I had, without knowing or planning it, learned to cheat on the movement. I was counterbalancing the lift by extending my hips backward, which accounted for lifting more weight with less results. Because of this experience, I developed a very good way to do the "good morning" exercise, producing tremendous results.

Make a wide belt that can be pulled up just above the knee on each thigh. This belt can be made of leather or some type of webbing, and should be about five to six inches wide. On each belt there should be a ring sewn in, or attached in some way just about midway of the width. By attaching a rope, chain, etc. to each of the rings and joining it to a single rope about three feet from the rings, you will have yourself an apparatus that will help you

perform the "good morning" exercise in a strict manner. Attach the rope that the two original ropes or chains are fastened to on to something stable that is just a little higher than the position that the belts are in around the thighs. When taking the "good morning" exercise weights from the squat racks, have enough length on the ropes so that you may step forward into your stance for the movement and tighten the rope. (Figures 29 and 30) Lean forward, do the exercise with tension being on the thigh belts. Keep a good footing so that you will not be apt to swing onto the belts and that way fall forward. To better explain, keep a great deal of weight on your feet and only use the belts as stabilizers to lean against and not swing all your weight on. This can best be done by using a very light weight for experimenting until you get it down pat.

Figure 29

Figure 30

There have been other such methods developed, such as leaning a board and different variations on such, but to me this is the best method I have used.

Do about ten of these "good morning" exercises for part of the set in this routine, and for the second portion I want you to get a weight that is almost your limit in the dead lift approaching it without hooks or straps, but use your regular competition grip and do one repetition. Put this weight down, stand erect, take several deep breaths and once again do a single. Continue doing this for ten repetitions. Try to do the lift as rapidly as possible, although I do not want you to sacrifice poundage for speed in performance.

During the first few times you try these singles, work up just how many breaths it takes between each lift. This way you can gauge your performance. Also try not to leave the original stance, keeping chalk nearby so that you can just pick it up and rechalk when necessary. These lifts will not only build strength but will really put your heavy dead lifts in the "groove."

Summing up this routine, do ten of the modified "good morning" exercises, ten of the heavy singles and you will have a set accomplished. This is another one of the real killers, so be conservative on your set, hoping to work up to three.

ROUTINE IV

I would like to start this routine by saying that there is no one that cannot dead lift more flat-footed than with the heels on their shoes. I say that I would like to start by making this statement, but there surely is an exception to every rule when it comes to lifting. This is because of the many body makeups and sizes of people. So, let us just say that, as a rule, there is no one who can't lift more flat-footed than with heels. I think this can be emphasized by many of the lifters who have caught on to what some are calling "dead lifting downhill." This expression describes those who would actually build up the front of their shoes raising the ball of the foot higher than the heel, so that when the dead lift is started, the lifter is really pulling back and has a better leverage on the bar, than if he was flat-footed or bare-footed.

Now operating under the assumption that being flat-footed is an advantage, let's take a great disadvantage. After a proper warm up, I would like for you to do a set of dead lifts with the first being in the regular form, the next four stiff-legged, and a final repetition going back down into your original regular dead lift stance and completing the lift. This is the only exercise in this routine I would like for you to do, performing four sets.

Do not misinterpret this as elementary, for we are going to do it the hard way. That is, with the heels elevated. I would like for you to elevate your heels just as high as possible and still be about to put weight on the entire foot. Maybe by wearing a shoe with a regular heel and putting it on top of a 2 x 4, there will be enough elevation. If this does not seem enough for you, put even more under the heel so that you are really lifting uphill instead of downhill. (Figures 31 and 32) This is going to put a unique strain on the entire dead lift movement, and should help overcome the sticking point that you personally have.

Figure 31

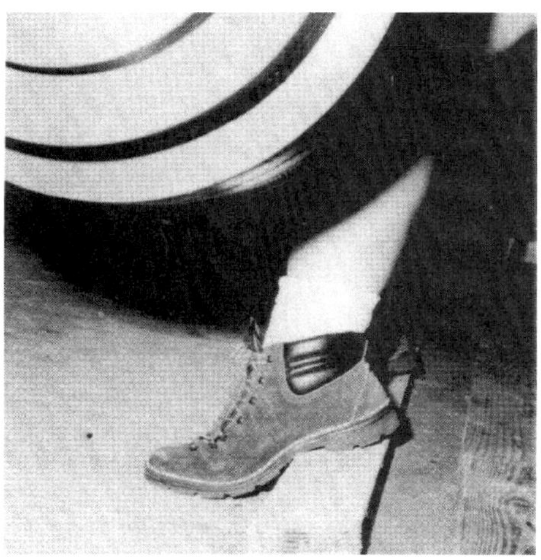

Figure 32

ROUTINE V

You're going to have to use your hooks or straps for this one. Here we are again to the "down movement." It's a little simpler with the dead lift, for your spotters will just have to help you up with the weight and then press down to force your movement. (Figure 33) Like in the bench press and the squat, you will have to give way at the very top, because even if the weight is many pounds over what you can dead lift, you can always sustain it at the up position. Prepare for the heavy down by doing the maximum reps in your dead lift, which we have said is eight. After the proper rest, your spotters are to give their help in bringing the heavier-than-you-can-manage weight to the finish position and as you voluntarily start to lower it, they will push down so that in no way you can stop the bar even though you should try with all your might. Repeat this four times. A set in this routine will be eight dead lifts, after warm up, and four repetitions in the down movement. If four repetitions are too many, cut them down, and even though you are working up to a hopeful three sets, judge this by your progress and endurance.

Figure 33

There are many lifting routines I can give you in every lift that is done in power lifting competition. A different combination of the routines I have instructed you in can be worked out by you as you advance and experiment on your own.

My tendency has always been to overtrain, and on occasions it has caught up with me just like it will with you. I point this out because some of

the routines I have given you are quite strenuous and some of you possibly cannot bear up under the full thrust of them. Even though I have said this many times throughout these instructions, play it cool, and work into them slowly.

Indeed, you will have to work hard to make progress in lifting as in any other thing in life. You will get out of this course just about what you put in. From many of my comments you should have gathered that weight lifting takes not only hard work to be successful, but also much thinking. I challenge you to THINK! Some of your best ideas will come when things are not going well. This is why I have offered you the possibilities of rearranging the lifts that I have recommended in the routines, or even rearranging the routines themselves where I have put them in sequence. First, I would like for you to try them as I have given them to you.

Yes, there are many other exercises that I could give you, but most of them take special equipment and as a rule, they are not any better than the ones I have projected. One is the inverted stiff-legged dead lift that I gave in "Secrets Of My Strength." This takes a bench, something like an incline board, but not quite as steep. The lift is done by the athlete hanging by his feed in an inverted position on this bench and pulling the bar from the starting to the finish position in the stiff-legged dead lift. The weights are attached by a cable hooked to the bar going up over the top end of the bench through a pulley. The weights themselves are, of course, suspended at the other end of the cable.

This is only an example of the many things that I have worked out through the years for special problems in lifting.

GOOD LUCK!